Interactive Press

Oh My Rapture

Gemma White is a poet living in Melbourne, Australia. Her first collection of poetry, *Furniture is Disappearing*, was published in 2014 by IP (http //ipoz.biz/ipstore). She shares her knowledge of poetry at http://www. gemmawhite.com.au, where she offers a free 5-day email poetry course. You can also sign up on her website to receive her e-newsletter for her latest writing news. Gemma has been published in many Australian literary magazines and journals, including *Best Australian Poems*. She also studied poetry at The University of Melbourne and The University of Edinburgh. You can read more of Gemma's poetry on Instagram (https:// www.instagram.com/bygemmawhite/) or Facebook (https://www.facebook.com/writingbygemma/).

Interactive Press
Brisbane

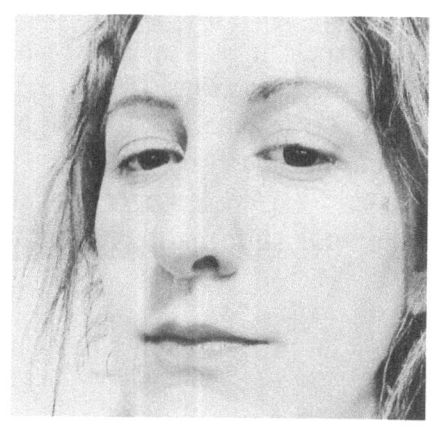

Oh My Rapture

Gemma White

Interactive Press

Interactive Press
an imprint of IP (Interactive Publications Pty Ltd)
Treetop Studio • 9 Kuhler Court
Carindale, Queensland, Australia 4152
sales@ipoz.biz
http://ipoz.biz/

Printed in 12 pt Adobe Caslon Pro on 14 pt Avenir Book.

ISBN: 978192830173 (PB); 978192830180 (Ebk)

A catalogue record for this
book is available from the
National Library of Australia

To Debbie, John, Kim, and Emma, my family,
and kindred spirits.

To the man with The Red Hand Files tattoo. Love you.

Acknowledgements

Cover design: Mikky Koopac
Book design: David P Reiter
Author Photo: Gemma White

Thanks to *Verity La* for publishing early versions of poems 10, 26, and 48. Thank you to my manuscript feedback council comprising Claire Gaskin, Henry Briffa, and Paul South. Special thanks to John L for his detailed attention to editing my work. These poems would not be what they are today without his help. Thanks to David Reiter and the team at IP, who believed in my work from the start. Thanks to Cassandra Atherton, Amanda Anastasi, Claire Gaskin, Matt Ryan, Henry Briffa, Nat O'Reilly, and Ali Whitelock for being willing to wax lyrical about my work on the back of the book and elsewhere. Thanks to Alexis Lateef for her support of my work. Thanks to Nick Cave and *The Red Hand Files*. Thanks to everyone who has bought or read one of my books, attended a book launch, reviewed one of my books, liked a post on Facebook or Instagram, or contacted me to tell of my book's impact on them. Thank you, thank you, thank you!

Contents

26	27
25	28
24	29
23	30
22	31
21	32
20	33
19	34
18	35
17	36
16	37
15	38
14	39
13	40
12	41
11	42
10	43
9	44
8	45
7	46
6	47
5	48
4	49
3	50
2	51
1	52

50

We start the fires
We bring the rain
We praise the sun
We lick every new frond
in our love of the infinite

We salivate over every flower
We drum the limbs alive
We lay naked underneath the sun
We kiss while standing in cool streams
We slap the waves with pleasure
as we roll right into the sands

We are here forever and
for just a moment combined
We awaken the skies
for we are sublime

49

i-text i-talk i-eat i-drink i-piss i-piss
i give no shits

i-take i-walk i-eat i-piss i-waste i-want i-buy
i buy

i-text i-pout
i-throw
shit out

i-come i-conquer
i wank

i-eat i-work i-buy i-jerk
i-waste i-want
i fuck

i-bin i-bin i-want-to-win
i-selfie i-drink
i try not to think

i-win i-win
i push away

i-vomit i-drink i-piss i-sleep
i-shit i-eat i-waste i-want
i pile more on

i-eat i-text i-talk i-talk
i-pout i-push i-try
i try

i-wish i-strain
i-vomit again
i-fuck it all up

i push you away

48

My madness is a burnt orange fox
Most of the time it is contained to its burrow
Occasionally it draws a crimson streak across life
Like a mandarin cloud at sunset
Its hues echo

47

Cat Power @ The Renfrew Ferry, April 25, 2007

oh beautiful she!
will you please come on now?
I've come all this way
please come on now!

where is she where is she where is she?
I've come here for her to see her for her!

does she have stage fright?
has she refused to come on stage
maybe?

where is she, where is she?
I've come all this way to see her now!

oh beautiful she!
will you please come on now?
she is coming on stage oh the glory
& oh she is here now she is god now she she she!

46

It is flying through the air
it's looking for the perfect time
and specific place
it's a ball of golden light
searching for the people
hunting for the moment
it might be finding you
or maybe the garbage man
only it knows and it's not telling
but it will land somewhere soft
creating a bridge from one to the other
warmth to you friend it says
you are not alone
we're in this together

45

messy	:	hair
blue	:	eyes
shared	:	songs
warm	:	skin
silent	:	hallway
open	:	door
dirty	:	sheets
you	:	

44

The closest thing it had to a scene was a retiree art gallery
whose paintings made me want to fall asleep
or commit a crime

Then there was the Geelong Fine Art Gallery
an oasis in a desert of sport where Robert taught me
the difference between acrylics and oils
and how they don't mix
just like how I didn't mix with the rest of the kids

But I felt safe there painting orange teapots
outlining women in Texta with mysterious green eyes

Some days I could even feel that my soul was still alive
Such a crappy small town

43

You create your world
perfectly in-line with your vegan values
For some reason this pisses me off

Your bathroom; organic towels, seashells
and a small blue boat
You don't even like me and I pretend
I don't mind

As for the living quarters
every wall covered in records, CDs, and films
You bring new meaning to the word *curated*
to the word *pretentious*, to the word *calculated*

I show you my songs
You tell me I'm too old to be any good

The critic has spoken but I don't mind
I don't like you anymore

Your vegan values, your perfect world
There's no room for me
So, I leave

42

I cannot stop objectifying
You're as erotic as an open wound
and your cigarettes smell like death on your breath

Who's to tell whose extinction I can smell
Yours, mine, does it matter?

I dream of a day where I can walk
in the sunlight of your thoughts
to a place of ferns and moss

Maybe someday they'll remove the razor from my mouth
until then my words are cutting and sharp
It seems extraction is the only answer

You're looking at me from the balcony of your thoughts
Your smoke screen hides an innocence
Please let me sleep in the shadow of your soul
So I can feel something again

41

Be volcanic rage
Be calm lagoon
Be rainforest
Be red parrot feather

Be cold moon
Be liquid sun
Be turquoise water
Be swimming turtle

Be every sand
Be the wind too
The howling, our howling
The burn, our burn

Be whispering leaves
Be trees that scream
Be the earthquake
Be the tender frond

Be honest, you're lying
Be honest, you're dreaming
And everything within and without
Waits for you to wake up

40

The dream was dressed in black fishnets The dream was too loud The dream was willed by my future self So yes it was scary So I put the dream on the bookshelf behind Patti Smith for safe keeping Where it still haunted me And then one day I took the dream down and tried it on and it still fit

I say:

I reclaim my dream even if it's too loud and willed by my future self Even if it's scary I will not put it back on the shelf Slowly, I begin to sing As every sorrow lifts As every hurt heals my dream is growing to fit my self as Patti Smith applauds from the bookshelf

39

for ease of transportation
I keep myself in a suitcase
it's small and suffocating
but I need the ease of transportation

one day no doubt I'll escape
but until that day
I'll tuck myself away
between the underwear
and the socks

they might wonder
where I've been all this time
how can I tell them?
I need the ease of transportation

allowing me to lock things up
keep it all together
folding away my feelings
like cotton shirts

until I burst out
propelled by emotion
jumping into freedom
clasping onto life

all turmoil
and unwashed clothing
no one was meant to see this

my insides scattered
like confetti sentiments

everything so visible
and open

38

I don't know how she knew
But she knew
She saw it in me
How I drew pictures from the age
I could pick up a pencil
One day she asked
If I wanted to do art classes

My mum has bipolar
And so do I

There is something
Sacred and healing
That happens when I write
When I paint
When I create songs
Maybe I am closer to God
Maybe the bad things can't find me here

37

where do you reside exactly is it somewhere above or inside?
are you thin like air or a thousand steps wide?
can you see us all the time?
what about when we're masturbating, what then?

is everything equally sacred and profane?
morals are slippery things you can slip to the wrong
side of the divide

but back to you God, back to you, I'm wondering
how you show yourself in a post-Madonna material world
is life like a BBC murder mystery where all the answers
arrive when we die?

can you hear me now?

if I lift my voice upwards, will you take my collect call?

hello?

36

love
sex sex
sex love sex sex love

love sex love love sex
sex love love sex sex love

oh darling oh sex sex love
oh darkly darling love love sex

oh yes sex love love sex
oh darling sex sex love

oh whisper now, in rapture now
oh sex sex love

music music sex and music
music music sex sex love
music, can you hear me music

sex sex sex love is coming

love is music filling me
music music sex sex love
ah ahh ahhh

oh my mystery, oh my darkness
oh my rapture, oh my music

35

we ain't making no allowances   we ain't ticking boxes
ain't filling in forms   ain't fitting in your size 8 miniskirts
ain't wearing suits or giving out our tax file numbers
this shit is real man, there's no time for pulling out a
parachute   no time for folding novelty socks   we got
guitars to shred   souls to save   we got mics and feedback
we got the real bad shit   ok   teach me something other
than how to point and shoot   so help me god

34

better not drink vodka yet
or I won't know wtf I'm doing up there

my strings buzz too much
they probably need changing, fuck

I worry what my fingers will do
on those slippery frets

here's the song with the falsetto bit
and even the falsetto bit
sounds ok tonight, thank fuck

now no-one is talking, they all go quiet
they're listening, quiet, so quiet

something is happening
when I let go and sing

33

The voice inside your head
is not your friend
and if the goal is to create
you must escape yourself
you must become a god
so far above that whiny self-pitying monologues
no longer exist
they have been left behind
along with unflattering selfies
black skinny jeans that no longer fit
and sneakers that let the rain in

32

you wrote to me in fifty different languages I love you
you kissed me in Dixons Recycled Music
you took my hand as we sat at a restaurant
you made me soup

you lay out on the grass with me as I looked at the sky
you looked at me like I was a goddess
you fucked me on the beach

you argued with me and we made up again
you called me with synchronicity
you said it was the end

31

I can go to heaven or hell to meet angels and devils
all in the same 24 hrs   if my mind inflames me   they
give me tablets to calm the fires   and I pray to all the
angels and devils that I don't become numb to the flames
when my mind inflames me I think of how your beauty
is surprising and creeps up on me   seeping into me like a
cooling ocean breeze   stopping the fire from getting too
hot and helping me to stay in and of this world   so that
when the spirit burns I can recover   and walk calmly by
your side once more

30

Losing you was not the tragedy
it was having lived a shuttered life
for so many years
before
you dumped me in the psych ward

29

If you build one more collection of modern grey boxes
where a beautiful house once stood
I will kill you, I'm not joking

Be dangerous, be like the plastic bag
everyone loves to hate them, but they're so damn useful

Politicians, everyone hates to love them
they're also dangerous, but not in the sexy way
that plastic bags are dangerous

Dishes tend to create division
and dishwashers make life easier
but they waste water and they're too expensive
you might just have to deal with it with your own hands
what a metaphor

Art is a reality TV mixtape
and road-rage is better than life
We've all been brainwashed by living
in the modern grey boxes
with only our chihuahuas for company

Let me tell you a story about plastic bags, little grey boxes
politicians and dirty dishes, it will be riveting, I promise

28

my imagination is a silver-blue
shimmering pool of worlds beneath the surface
sometimes
I'm afraid to jump

the voices in my head say
you'll drown in there

but my mind was made to heal me
it knows more than it lets on

there is a willow tree above my pool
it grows slowly and shelters me

after I emerge to take out the rubbish
I can sleep wise and deep
with my willow tree looking over me

27

It is now when I'm kissing you
How could it be any other time?
Tomorrow, the smell of your hair on my pillow
I will designate you mine
I made my decision while we were kissing
It will surface from my unconscious
And I will call it tomorrow's declaration
Of war on boredom
Of faith in love
Of the possibility of more kissing

26

I have a condition, an indoctrination
that gives me mysterious abilities
some people call it an illness

I have seen things no-one else has seen
heard things that "are not there"
my life has been poorer and richer for it

At the beginning it was all fear but sometimes ecstasy
a bold feeling of power, a united expression of love
other times I'd cry, still believing the stories in my head

These days I try not to get tricked
being sane is more boring
but it's also more comforting

Now I look for magic in the morning commute
I take my pills morning and night
and the mysteries are kept at bay

25

to be a good poet:

    use metaphors, similes and all the rest
    allude to Greek mythology or make an obvious
    & safe comment on contemporary society

to be a good poet:

    be so dense they'll need a dictionary
    be clever and cut off from the body
    never use abstract nouns
    don't attempt humour!

to be a good poet:

    write in forms that are centuries old
    be aloof and self-consciously obscure
    shroud your meaning in secrecy
    make editors wet with your vagueness

but:

    I don't want to be a good poet
    I want to be a naughty one!

24

it starts   with a few lines   maybe two

and perhaps   a tune

i write the words out on some paper

record the tune on my phone   before it can get away

my chords are usually simple

maybe one day   i'll get better at this   but for today

my simple songs   are good enough

23

I don't have the answer for you, maybe I'm not meant to
when you're in the dark, a lightbulb can seem so far away

People tell you to flip the switch as if that is the key
but all this advice makes you feel worse
like it's your fault for having feelings

I don't have the answer for you but I'm here and I care
what I know from life is that things always change

Gradually then quickly again and again

22

A.I. writing a song that's perfect
for the human consciousness
is like a vibrator that's perfect
for the female anatomy
it might do the job at hand, but something is lost
in the connection

21

The creeping feeling of happiness

Comes upon us unexpected

I have your soul in my hands as you have mine

Will we be good guardians?

Will we be gentle and kind?

Will we execute our ideas of love, one by one?

And in the firing squad

Will we find something tangible and real, like blood?

20

the day I sang out of tune
I don't actually remember what I did in the morning

the day I sang out of tune I'd asked my boyfriend to be there
because I was a little nervous

the day I sang out of tune we got there early
I had a vodka and watched other people sing

the day I sang out of tune
time ticked on until it was my turn

I don't think I sang out of tune at the start
but I couldn't hear anything so I tried to sing louder

my voice, not used to this, broke several times
I thought Jesus this is a disaster

but I couldn't stop singing, singing with all my verve
with all my courage, I sang out of tune

when the song was over, I slunk off the stage
out of tune with the world

19

Sweet flowers nodding scented tubes in spring
carpeting lands with screaming fans
Hyacinthoides non-scripta aka Nickeus Caveus
popular & flourishing in the British Isles

A common bluebell or simply Saint Nick
of the rock and roll

Commanding the stage to infuse a blue mood
into the ripe earth of his listeners' minds
flowering into meaning the experience
the transcendence, the uncommon, the primal, perennial

18

sitting in the tree in my parent's backyard
the one that hangs over the muddy pond
listening to the echoes and screams of kids in the park
the doves cooing from the rafters of my parent's house

it's sunny out here in the afternoon
the leaves make shadow patterns on my clothes and face
I wouldn't want to be 10 again
but this moment is okay

17

i'd rather

a. go swimming
b. masturbate
c. touch my lover on the clavicle
d. kiss my arse goodbye
e. make a wish on a dandelion
f. freak out
g. write a stupid poem
h. crack the crap out of my back
i. pray like my life depended on it
j. pat a furry animal
k. sleep
l. cuddle a tree trunk
m. paint my nails vampire black
n. lick melting ice-cream from my fingers
o. fill my face with strawberry donuts
p. fuck anyone who happens to be nearby
q. laugh hysterically – at something that isn't funny
r. dump a really good shit
s. sip my least favourite alcoholic drink
t. give a full-bodied embrace
u. wear my Sunday best to prepare for what's to come
v. pretend I'm enamoured with humanity
w. drive to no destination
x. have my feet licked
y. make public nudity a constant practice
z. congratulate myself on having made it this far

16

an ending (ascent) – Brian Eno
lay lady lay – Bob Dylan
we float – PJ Harvey
famous blue raincoat – Leonard Cohen
anthrocene – Nick Cave & The Bad Seeds
don't be shy – Cat Stevens
free – Cat Power
open heart surgery – Brian Jonestown Massacre
the killing moon – Echo and the Bunnymen
gloria – Patti Smith

15

whether we were together or apart it didn't matter
because we were linked across the ether

whether we are together or apart it doesn't matter
because your heart sleeps inside mine

even as we hug other bodies, even as we love other souls
something remains, something of you remains

14

they don't know what kind of art you should make
what kind of words you should create
they don't have the right kind of eyes

you can be sure they won't recognise you
on that day when you stand brave and strong
and declare your cosmos done

13

there is a song for this that they will make you sing
but please try not to join in the chorus
for that will make you one of them

the tune is so damn catchy
notes like arrows point to the accused
and musicians fall like dropped names

today you must stand unyielding
not complicit in the weaponising
silence is your saviour

when the core of the anthem stinks
don't start humming
stand in your own quiet revolution

there's a song playing in the background
we'd turn it off if we could hear it still

12

I'm not looking for a one-night thing

I'm not even looking for a fling

I want someone who means something

Someone with soul

Someone who's not too young or too old

Someone without pressure

But with a point

It's not that I don't want to put effort in

It's just that impressing people is exhausting

So, I'm not looking for a one-night thing

I want the kind of love where your eyes lock

Where you acclimatise to their body as home

Where their phone calls anticipate your thoughts

11

What a relief, I do not know

I do not have everything out in a row

I love that phrase, I do not know

Imagine politics – We do not know

Imagine medicine – We do not know

Imagine religion – We do not know

Thank God someone's pretending to keep us all safe

For what would happen if we all admitted

We do not know

10

We do not show our ideas to just anyone

We do not boast of our plans to unbelievers

We put on our black skirts and suits

Every morning is a chance to do our work in confidence

We could be ordinary folk with a job to do in our

Cosmic costumes

We could be artists, chameleons with serious

Metaphysical intent

We could be on the train or behind you in line

We do not show you who we are

We disappear at will

And only later do you see what we've left behind

9

Dear Nick C   I'm ashamed to write to you   I'm not
worthy I'll never be that washed in moonlight I'll never
be a dark bottomless gothic pool I don't even have black
hair I want to be the wishing well that one of your song
characters throws a corpse into – his freshly murdered
lover's hair still tangled with blood How do people talk
to their music gods   I wish I could be cool about this
But in truth I'm all panting tongue when I want to be
slinky feline silhouette   I feel like I am looking up at a
giant with elongated arms and legs   It's too upsetting
But I'm writing to say thank-you Because I'm an artist
too   And something in what you've created really got
through to me It really got through

8

If I lost you I would howl a long and visceral sound
people would hear the scream and shudder
the sky, all pink brushstrokes

I'm standing on the bridge
mothers, turn your children away

If I lost you the owls would leave their nests
the hyenas would stop laughing
the wolves would join me in silhouette
howling in sympathy

7

Sometimes my chest thuds so loud
I cannot hear a thing

Words are free to frame
by any gymnastics of lexicon

Anyone can argue
but no-one wants to listen

When my passions rise
I can be so righteous

How can we learn
to live with one another

With full understanding of what it means
without abdicating our own selves

My mouth hungers for revenge
but now I wait for his truth

Knowing that there is more to it
seeking to appreciate

A different point of view

6

I didn't know you would leave so soon

that 60th wedding anniversary I didn't attend

so close to the end

5

When I hug you
I imagine that the whole world stops
all the trains, buses and trams
pause in their tracks

People in workplaces
at lunchtime stop with their mouths suspended
around a ham and mayo sandwich

Others halt while reaching
for carrots and turnips standing frozen
in the vegetable section

We are gods in this single second of bliss
floating on infinity until there is nothing left

4

It's sending psychic messages 24/7
so nothing feels quite right
You're washed in a quiet dread

The thing you're not doing knows you
and it's sending psychic messages 24/7

Not because you want world domination
Not because you want to be laid more
Not even because you want to be adored

But because this is your destiny
this is your place in the world

3

I want to move like a queen   who doesn't need to command

who holds onto herself in any situation   who won't blame you or anyone

because whatever happens   the queen knows exactly what her next move will be

2

I love dachshunds
I just can't help it
They're so damn little and cute
Their legs working overtime to catch up
I'm sure if I had one
It would be a little prick
I've heard they are
It would probably bark all the time
Steal sausages off the kitchen bench
Devour chocolate in a perverted cry for help
That resulted in all my money going in vet bills
And when I walked it
Everyone would want a pat
Little do they know
What a cunning bastard
They are petting
Little would they know
Until they got
Their own cunning bastard
Barking all the time
Stealing sausages etc
That's how dachshunds
Ensure the propagation
Of their species
Strategic little buggers

1

We are buildings without windows, trains
stopped dead on tracks that permit no surprises
Until death do us part, until death do us part
Until death do us

Have you seen a rainbow recently?
There's something about music, a song I used to know
How did it go?

We are buildings racing into clouds, trains
that toot too loud for humility

Have you seen a rainbow recently?
There's something about music, a song I used to know

How did it go?

After reading this book, please accept this invitation to share your honest feedback on Amazon, Goodreads, the Interactive Publications website (http://ipoz.biz), and anywhere else that takes your fancy. You can also email the author at gemmawhite.com.au or sign up for her newsletter there.